Blind Date

Kristin Birke

Copyright © 2024 by Kristin Birke

All rights reserved.

No portion of this book may be reproduced in any form without written permission from the publisher or author, except as permitted by U.S. copyright law.

Contents

1. Part 1 — 1
2. Part 2 — 4
3. Part 3 — 7
4. Part 4 — 18
5. Part 5 — 21
6. Part 6 — 26
7. Part 7 — 31
8. Part 8 — 38
9. Part 9 — 43
10. Part 10 — 50
11. Part 11 (I Fell in love with my Best Friend) — 58
12. Part 12 — 63
13. Part 13 — 70

14.	Part 14 (Way too much sex)	74
15.	Part 15	82
16.	The Final Chapter	88

Part 1

The door to the restaurant had a vague mirror-like quality and I stopped to look at my reflection before walking in.

My stomach was flipping over itself and I was nervous to even attempt to gauge how I looked. It had been a very long time since I had been on a first date (or any date, really) and I had never been on a blind date before. I was so nervous that I leaned one hand on the side of the wall to keep myself steady as I inspected myself.

Unfortunately, I saw exactly what I expected to see. A mess!

I'd walked twenty blocks from my apartment ("it's a nice night!" I said to myself, "and I am early, might as well walk." Moron) and my hair hadn't stood up well. I kept my black hair long and had straightened it before I left, but it was a getting frizzy from the humid air. My eye shadow, which had looked smoky when I put it on at the apartment, looked a little raccoonish now around my large, green eyes. I have exceptionally pale skin and so, in my apartment, I'd tried to redden my cheeks a bit. Now I found in the natural light that I'd put it on too thickly, looking a bit whorish. Somehow, the bright color made my aquiline nose look even bigger than usual. At least my teeth were white.

Below my neck, the situation was even worse. I had debated a long time about what, exactly, I should wear. I'd tried on several dresses, ranging from conservative to slutty. But I finally decided that none of them worked. I'd put on a suit I often wore to work because I liked the way it made my ass look. But now, looking at myself in the reflection, I found I looked far too professional for an evening dinner date. The suit was form fitting with a short coat and tight pants, but it still looked like I was preparing to meet clients. My small feet were clad in flats that didn't exactly scream "I am ready to date." Worse, for some reason I'd buttoned my shirt all the way up to my throat. I AM A GENIUS! I quickly pulled out some tissues and dialed back the makeup on my face, giving it more even look around my eyes and cheeks. I also used a corner of a tissue to straighten up my deep red lip stick. I didn't want to whip a brush out in the middle of the street or anything, so I just patted my hair down as best I could. Finally, I self-consciously unbuttoned the top two buttons blouse, exposing the tops of my breasts. I looked into the half-reflection of the door again and saw, once again, what I expected to see: a desperate 5'3, 138lbs, 34-year old woman who hadn't been on a date in six months and hadn't been fucked in nearly a year. But hey, at least my make-up looked better. I took a deep breath and pushed the door open.

Part 2

The restaurant was dimly lit and with what appeared to be bare bulbs hanging down on wires from the 15 foot ceilings. I looked around the room and saw that the dining area was very deep and narrow. I looked in the back of the room and saw a wave-shaped bar against the back wall, it was also dimly lit, though it had a somewhat green color. There were tables against both side walls, so that one person would sit on a chair facing the wall and another person in a booth seat across from them. There was a narrow hallway down the middle between the backs of all the chairs. The door entered on the right, front side of this dining room and the hostess' stand was directly in front. I looked to my left as I walked in and saw one booth against the large window pane in front of the restaurant. The hostess smiled at me. "Good evening, welcome to Apple, do you have a reservation?" she asked sweetly. This was, by far, the trendiest restaurant I'd been in since I'd entered my thirties. I looked around the room and saw a large crowd of hip people talking quietly. How had Kim and Eric thought this place would fit me? If I was going on a date with someone who would like this place, how could he fit me? "I uh...I am meeting someone here. My friends said you'd be aware..." I said. God, was there anything more mortifying than that? 'Hello, I am a grown woman going on a blind date; I was told this restaurant had a separate "desperation" section with a separate ventilation system...' "Oh, you're one of Kim's friends," the hostess said and I blushed, "How is she doing?" "Fine," I said awkwardly. Glad to be the center of attention here. "She used to bartend her like two years ago, I hadn't heard from her for a while before she called to set up this reservation," she explained. I had forgotten that my close friend Kim had taken up bartending for a couple of months after she quit teaching and before she became an accountant. "Oh yeah..." I said. Not certain what I was supposed to ad. "So are you Ash or Riley?" She asked. "Oh, uh..." I said, I hadn't expected that. I hadn't known my date's name. I was just told to show up at a time and what to say to the hostess. But it was surprising that we both happened to have androgynous names. I suppose either Ash or Riley could be a man's name, or a woman's name, "I am Ash." "Well you are the first one here, let me show you to your seat," the hostess said. She grabbed two menus and a wine list. She quickly moved from behind the stand and beckoned for me to follow. She led me right to the booth in the window. She pointed to the seat where my back would be to the door and I sat down. "Thank you," I said nervously. "When you date arrived I will show them to the table," she said then she turned and left. I slunk down in the booth and looked at my watch. It was already 5 minutes after 9. I thought I was going to be late. Maybe "Riley" was blowing me off and I could go home and watch television in my pajamas like a normal, happy Friday night.

Part 3

How had I let Kim and Eric talk me into this? Kim and I had gone to college together, freshman roommates in fact. She was pretty much the only person from college I kept in touch with. She was still my best friend in the city, maybe in the world. And Eric was her husband, they'd met junior year. I hadn't liked him much at first, but he'd grown on me. All of that was to say that they'd both known me for around 15 years. They knew I'd been more relieved than anything when I'd decided to give up on dating six months ago. Kim, and I suppose Eric, had heard all of my horror stories about deadbeat boyfriends and awful dates.

Yet here I was, sitting in a booth waiting for some guy named "Riley" from Eric's office to show up. I had resisted this date for three solid weeks. I remember the first time it came up, Kim and I were sitting on the couch at her place, Eric wasn't yet home from the office.

"So, what are you doing this weekend?" She'd asked and I'd snorted.

"Working, were you under the impression I get weekends?" I asked. I worked around 70 hours a week, usually ten hours a day, every day.

"It is supposed to be nice out this week, you should take a day off, relax," Kim had said. She kept her eyes on the television, but I saw her look at me out of the corner of her field of vision, gauging me.

"I don't have the time," I said. Now it was Kim's turn to snort.

"You've been at that office since you graduated from business school and you've never taken a day off. You must have a solid month of personal leave and a month of sick leave all saved up," she said. Actually, it was a lot more than that. But I liked to be busy and liked to work. Besides, what did she care if I didn't take my sick days?

"Yeah well, there is a lot to do this week. They really can't be without me this weekend," I said in a voice that indicated I didn't want to talk about this.

"So said every office drone ever!" Kim shot back. I turned and looked at her now and she turned too.

"What?" I asked.

"What what?" she asked.

"Why do you want me out of the office on Saturday? This isn't another ill-fated surprise birthday party is it?" I asked, referring to a notorious event ten years earlier in which no one except for Eric had showed up for my surprise party. Not even me. Everyone stuck in traffic. Kim laughed, probably remembering that day.

"No, it isn't even your birthday for a month."

"That's what makes it a surprise," I replied.

"No," Kim said, getting a little more serious now, "In all honesty, Eric said there is someone at his office who he thinks would be absolutely perfect for you and..."

"No, thank you, but no," I'd said.

"Come on," Kim said, inching closer to me on the couch, "Consider it a favor to Eric."

"Eric owes me six favors already remember? Three trips to the airport, babysitting your son twice, and babysitting your dog once," I noted.

"Then as a favor to me, he said this person would be perfect for you. It could be fun," she said.

"No," I'd said again.

"Come on, just hear me out," she'd pleaded. I found it sort of off putting and I decided to put an end to it.

"I don't want to talk about it," I said, loudly and rudely and then I turned back to the television and made it very clear that the conversation was over. And with that she'd dropped it. But every night for the next two weeks when I saw her, or spoke with her on the phone, she'd gently broached the subject again. She'd be quiet about it whenever I told her to drop it, but she'd always find a way to bring it back up again. She was really driving me insane.

It was about two weeks to the day that I'd finally caved, but not without a fight. We were sitting on the couch again, but both of us were drinking coffee and just chitchatting about our days. Suddenly, Kim became quiet. It was clear she wasn't listening to what I was saying anymore. It looked like she was summoning her strength for something. Kim took a deep breath and let out a sigh.

"Ash," she said and I looked over at her, she refused to make eye contact, "You know that I love you and I am always going to love you," she said. I felt my heart quicken. My mouth went dry and my palms got wet. I was nervous. This sounded like the start of a bad conversation. What was she going to say?

"What? Is something wrong?"

"I am worried about you," she said finally, "And I can't sit by and let this happen anymore. I love you and want you to do what makes you happy, but I can't sit by while you choose to be miserable," she explained. I felt like I'd been slapped. I had not expected that. I put my hands up and shook my head.

"I am happy Kim, really. Happier than I ever was when I was dating," I explained, feeling defensive. Kim had never questioned my life choices before, just like I didn't question hers. If she wanted to marry and have a boatload of kids, more power to her. If I wanted to be alone and focus on my work, that was my choice.

"Ash I know you. You are not happy. You haven't been happy in a long time," she said. I could see tears in the corner of her eye and I felt my defensiveness fade. Even if she was wrong (and I told myself that she was totally, TOTALLY wrong), she at least was being sincere.

"I am happier than when I was with Todd," I said, referring to my most recent serious boyfriend (and the last person I'd slept with).

"Well yeah, that isn't saying much," Kim said, "I think that you always date...the wrong kind of people...and are miserable, that you think the absence of misery is happiness." Now she looked up, her eyes slightly red. I felt a pang, Kim had touched on something. I felt a shiver.

"I am good," I said, my voice sounding small and cracking.

"Ash, how often do we see each other? How often do we talk?" she asked suddenly seeming to change the subject.

"Every day I guess," I said sheepishly and she nodded.

"At least once, usually two or three times a day. You are here almost every single day, even if we talk on the phone twice while you're at work," she said.

"We are best friends; that's what best friends do," I said, wondering what she was getting at.

"We are not best friends," she said and I felt the wind come out of me. Not best friends? What the hell did that mean? One minute we were talking about some stupid blind date and the next we were talking about...what? Not being friends.

"We..." I started, feeling sluggish and off-kilter, but Kim put her hand up.

"I am your best friend. And you are my best female friend, the person I go to when I need someone outside of my marriage to talk to. You were the maid of honor at my wedding. We have a very special bond and I recognize that. We had it when we first met. We will always have that. But Eric is my best friend," she said, and I her words came out choked, like it was hurting her to say this. I felt my cheeks getting red, embarrassed and angry at myself. I hadn't expected that.

"I never meant to like...insert myself into your marriage; I wasn't trying to be a third wheel or something..." I stumbled. I felt myself crying now. I felt so stupid. All this time, Eric and Kim were resenting me, wishing I would go away. And there I was, oblivious to how annoying and intrusive I was.

"Oh please Ash, you know that isn't what I mean," Kim said, actually sounding angry at me, "I love you and Eric loves you. We like that you are around all the time, we like that Steven has an 'aunt' who is with him all the time. Don't be stupid. I am not telling you to butt out or something, it isn't about that." Now I was more confused than ever.

"Then what are you saying?"

"I am saying...I am saying that you need something more in your life that what you have," she said. She reached forward on the couch and grabbed my hands. She looked deeply into my eyes. I was so confused and still embarrassed but I found comfort in my friend's touch. I could feel her affection for me and see love in her eyes, "I am not talking about my needs or my...whatever. I am not talking about me. You. I can tell, and Eric can tell, that you are not happy. You are not miserable anymore, but you aren't happy. You are grasping for something here, with me, that my family and I just cannot provide for you. You need intimacy, and I don't mean sex. You need... you need more than I can give you as your best friend. You need to love someone and be loved by someone on a level that you don't have. You need what I have with Eric."

I felt myself getting angry again. Of course I'd compared my life to Kim and Eric's life together in the past and found it...less fulfilling by comparison. And yes I wanted something that they had, but it wasn't Kim's place to tell me that. It wasn't her place to rub it into my face that I was less complete than she was. I resented it and I stood up quickly to leave her house.

"Ash..."

"I am not some pathetic loser..."

"Ash, honey that isn't what I am..."

"I don't need what you have, just because what you have makes you happy, doesn't mean that everyone wants it or needs it..."

"I am sorry," she said suddenly, "I said it all wrong. I know that. Trust me, I definitely wasn't trying to say anything more than...please stop and listen." I had been moving towards her door but I stopped.

"Okay," I said coldly, deciding to give her one last chance.

"I am not saying that I have the key to happiness and you just need to follow my example and you will get it. I am saying that...I think you want a romantic relationship whether you know it or not. I think you want something that you don't even know that you want and cannot understand. In the same way you knew I was pregnant before I did, before the test knew, because you know me so well. I know this because I love you. I am saying this for the sake of that connection; I want you to trust me. And if you go on this date and you feel less happy with this person from Eric's work than you do here with us, then you come back and we forget I ever said anything. I will admit I was wrong, and that will end it. But do me this favor."

I looked at Kim on the couch. She was leaning towards me, her face was absolutely earnest. While I knew she was wrong about me, I also knew that she thought she was looking out for me. I felt my anger fall, replaced by a little bit of embarrassment, but also a potent love for my friend. She always looked out for me, how could I need anything more in my life? But I knew she was hurting. Hurting for me, even if she had no business doing so. I was touched. And I wanted to stop her suffering.

"One date?" I asked.

"Only have to commit to one," she said, her face relaxing, she knew I was in.

"Okay," I mumbled and she smiled widely, making me smile in return.

"Thank you," she said, "But trust me, in a couple of days, you'll be thanking me."

"I doubt it," I'd said.

Part 4

Now, sitting in the booth in "Apples," nervously playing with my bread knife, I found that my prediction was, unfortunately, extremely accurate. If things kept up this way, I would not be thanking anyone for any of this. At least my obligation would be discharged. I'd never have to go through this nonsense again. I looked at my watch again. Another ten minutes had passed. I resolved that Riley didn't arrive in three minutes I was going to leave. I kept my eyes down on the clock, willing it forward until I reached my excused time. With just thirty seconds left, I heard hostesses voice.

"Right here," she said and I felt my heart jump into my throat. So close to getting out of this, but now my date was here. I looked up as a person flopped into the seat across me.

"I am so sorry," she said, "I could get a c...oh...I am sorry... must be the wrong table." It was, I was shocked to find, a woman sitting across from me. Clearly, more than one date was going on tonight and the hostess had made a pretty blatant error.

"Yeah uh..." I said, "I am waiting on a blind date..." I looked to find the hostess, but she had already walked away.

"Me too," the woman said. She was a good deal younger than me; I estimated she was around 25 years old. She didn't exactly look like she was prepared for a date, though I had to admit she looked much prettier than me. She was around the same height as me, but much thinner. While I had a voluptuous build (or doughy if you ask me on a day when I am not feeling so hot about myself), she was rail thin. I estimated she weighed around 105lbs. She was wearing a tight white t-shirt with black lettering that said "The Clash" and a pair of skin-tight black jeans. She had small, perky breasts that sat up high in her t-shirt, a flat stomach, somewhat narrow hips, and thin legs. I noticed (for some reason) that she had small, delicate hands that clasped her iphone and her fingernails were painted black. She had pale white skin, thick pink lips, a small pixie nose and bright, massive blue eyes. Her make-up was kind of intense though applied with some skill. Most strikingly perhaps, she had messy dirty-blonde hair underneath a trendy black hat. And when I say messy, I mean it had a strong rat's nest appearance. Though, somehow given her general appearance, it actually kind of worked.

I laughed a little to myself, not exactly the tall, dark and handsome date I'd expected. "I guess the restaurant made a mistake, we will get it sorted out when the waitress comes," I said. The girl nodded. She gave me an awkward smile, pretty and toothy.

"I should've figured something like this would happen, my luck," the woman said and shrugged her shoulders. She sort of stretched out a bit, looking a bit tired. She arched her back into the booth, pressing her breasts forward against her tight shirt, and then leaned back.

"Oh I know, I told my friend this was going to happen. Well, I mean not this exactly, but something bad," I said and the woman nodded.

Part 5

"Your friend the one who set you up?" she asked.

"Yeah, how about you?"

"Oh some guy I work with," she said. There didn't really seem to be anything else to say. I looked across at her for a moment, felt self-conscious, and then looked away. She seemed a bit embarrassed too. Though, to be honest, the fact that she was in the same predicament made me feel a little better. She was a very attractive girl, so maybe a blind date wasn't just for pathetic, old people.

"Maybe our dates are sitting together at some other table," she said after a long awkward pause. I laughed, a little more forcefully than I intended, trying to sound casual.

"I think you'd have heard by now," I said, "Guys would be...less understanding. I think our boys are late." I explained.

"Yeah, a little uptight," she said and we both uncomfortably nodded together. There was silence for nearly a minute after that. I looked at the pattern on the tablecloth. I heard her hand tapping on the seat next to her.

"Well at least it is a nice night for a date...if they ever show up," I said, looking out the window.

"Yeah..." she said. It was very dark already, but the moon was full, casting a pale blue light on the street outside the restaurant. People shuffled by slowly and each youngish man who walked passed raised the possibility that prince charming was here.

"Well...you look really nice for your date," I said. I didn't really know what else to say and the silence was making me tense. She smiled.

"Thanks...I never know how to dress for dates. I feel like I look, I don't know, trashy," She laughed, "but I guess I am a little trashy. You look pretty too, you're going to wow him." I knew that she was just talking for the sake of noise, like me, but it was nice to get a compliment.

"I felt too business-like," I said.

"Well it suits you," she replied and I didn't know if that was a good thing.

"Well you don't look trashy, you look...at ease. And it suits you," I said returning the compliment. We smiled at one another and then lapsed again into silence, but we felt a little less strange now. At least we weren't complete strangers anymore. But soon, that silence stretched out too. Where was that waitress? Finally, the woman sighed.

"Even the men who aren't in my life yet aren't reliable," she joked and I smiled back in response.

"Well look at it this way," I said, "Everything that could go wrong at this point has. At least we are due for some good luck."

"Ugh," she said, "I had a concert tonight and I cancelled for this date! Things had better go really damn right after this."

"I was supposed to be working," I commiserated. She shook her hair, letting her wild hair wave, and then picked her cell phone off the table.

"The guy who set me up said my date was like...anally retentively prompt. This is pissing me off," and then she lifted up her phone toward her face and started to flip through it. "Maybe I will text him, Eric is a bit absent-minded, he may have given me the wrong place." I felt a sudden stab and looked more closely at the girl. Had she said...Eric? Did she look like the kind of person who would work at...a record label? That couldn't be right. What a weird coincidence. I realized that I was lacking some very important information about this woman.

"What's the name of your date?"

"Oh the hostess just said, I'm looking for some guy named Ash. Like the Evil Dead, I guess. Weird name," she said, flipping through her contacts. I felt the world spin a bit.

"Riley?" I asked and she looked up from her phone. One of her eyebrows was raised.

"Yes?" she asked and that confirmed it. I felt like I couldn't breathe. What the hell was going on here?

"Hi, I am Ash. Short for Ashley, but please call me Ash" I said, extending my hand. I sounded wooden and choked, but I didn't know what else to do. Riley's mouth dropped open; she smiled nervously, and shook her head. We both realized what this meant. Our "boys" weren't late. Both our dates had been on time.

"Uh...No, I...I am looking for a man," she explained. I blushed. I felt so stupid.

Part 6

"Eric Carter and Hot Kim?" she asked, shaking me out of my thoughts.

"Yeah Eric and Kim Carter," I said, but her phrasing seemed strange, "Hot Kim?" I asked. Riley's face was extremely red and she was looking down at her phone, avoiding my eyes.

"Oh uh, yeah. There are two guys in department with wives named 'Kim' so we call one 'tall Kim' because she is taller than her husband, Hank, and the other one 'Hot Kim' because she is so...hot and Eric is such a dork. Some of the other guys made it up," she said absentmindedly. Well we were definitely set up together. Eric and Kim had set me up with a woman named Riley from Eric's office. They knew

I was a straight woman. They apparently knew Riley was a straight woman. And they did this to us. Why?

"This is so embarrassing, I am so sorry" I mumbled but Riley didn't say anything. I don't know why I apologized; it felt like something to do. Something real to do. For a minute we sat in complete silence, too uncomfortable to speak. What the hell was all this supposed to mean? I tried to focus on one idea, to try to place this situation in frame where it would make sense. All I could tell was that I was absolutely mortified. And I could only come to one conclusion.

"This is not a funny joke, I didn't think Eric was such a dick," Riley said, apparently reaching the same conclusion I had. This was some sort of elaborate practical joke. Maybe Riley had been single for a while too, so they set us up to make us feel...I don't know. Stupid? It didn't make any sense. But none of this made any sense. I wasn't a lesbian. Why would Eric and Kim think this was funny? God, this was just the most humiliating thing ever.

"It isn't like them..." I said finally, but without conviction. What else could this mean? Maybe they had sat us next to the window so they could look in at us and laugh. I looked out the window but didn't see anyone I recognized in the street.

"Well here we fucking are!" Riley snapped. I felt the heat of her anger and quailed. I must've made a face, "Sorry. Not your fault. Just feel really conspicuous. Everyone thinks we are on a date or something. The whole wait staff is probably in on this joke. And honestly I am uncomfortable with you seeing me this...uncomfortable."

"I am in the same boat, you don't need to be embarrassed with me," I said. I was still just trying to get a handle on my ideas. Beyond the same embarrassment I was trying to talk Riley out of, I couldn't begin to register my own emotions.

"Hi, I am Heather, I am going to be your waitress tonight," a voice finally said. Riley and I turned and looked at a cute young girl in a black shirt and tie smiling brightly, "Would you like a bottle of wine or something else to drink to get started." I felt flustered. The last thing that I wanted was to leave.

"No...uh, thank you but no," I said, stumbling out the words. But I suddenly knew what I wanted to do, "We changed our minds. We are going to go." I explained. Riley nodded without looking at the waitress and grabbed her purse, ready to go. She apparently agreed. The joke was over. The waitress put her hands on her hips, tilted her head to the side, and bit her lip.

"Oh, I am sorry to hear that," the waitress said, "What should I tell Kim about the bill?" I felt so strange, hearing her reference Kim.

"Kim? What does it matter to her?" Riley spat.

"There is no bill, we haven't ordered anything, we are just going to go," I said, starting to stand up.

"Oh I know, I mean the agreement," she said.

"What agreement," I asked, stopping. What other joke was there. Some sort of wedding cake or something? 'Look at those two women who can't get men. Might as well just buy them a dozen cats and put them together.' Funny stuff.

"Kim and her husband, they agreed to pay your dinner tonight. Should I let her know that you don't want it? Or what?" The waitress asked. I didn't care if Kim and Eric agreed to pay the mortgage on my condo, I was done.

"I don't care, I just want to go."

"How much did they agree to pay," Riley said, sitting back down in her chair. The waitress shrugged. I was reaching back into the seat to grab my purse. I stopped moving as there was something different now in Riley's voice.

Part 7

"Oh they didn't say, they just said they'd get the bill. They left their credit card on file," the waitress explained. Riley looked over at me. A broad smile spreading out across her face, making her look devious (and pretty). She leaned forward on the table, placing her elbows on the surface and rubbing her hands together.

"Is that a fact?" she asked. The waitress nodded, looking a bit confused. Riley turned back towards me, "You thinking what I am thinking?" she said, her voice sounding low and malicious. I instantly surmised what she was hinting at. A little bit of revenge. My humiliation in exchange for a very, very expensive meal. For a second I thought about it, but I started to shake my head.

"No, I can't, they..." I started.

"Want us to have a good meal," Riley said, smiling sweetly at the waitress, then she turned towards me, raising bother her eyebrows and speaking slowly, "I am in payroll, trust me Eric can handle it. And they DESERVE to hear about US being happy," she said, each word dripping with meaning. I knew she was right, but I was about to demur again.

I was angry at Eric and Kim, and confused, but I couldn't do that. It was wrong to take someone's money. Especially a friend. Even if that friend was being...weirdly cruel without provocation. But thinking about that strange spite from my friends, and hearing about what I deserved and about being happy, I thought about my conversation with Kim. The one where she'd cried and told me about me about my future and my needs. I thought about the emotional ups and downs of that conversation, the way that Kim seemed to really hurt for me. The fact that I sacrificed what I wanted just to make her happy.

It was all for this...joke or prank. And I got what, a free meal out of it? Hardly even. Each memory, the feelings and guilt she'd stirred in me, heightened the rage. I had never felt so angry in my entire life.

"Actually, I am feeling pretty hungry," I said, sitting back down in the seat. Eric and Kim were going to pay until we were equal and then pay some more. Then I might not ever speak to them again. This was unforgiveable. A joke in bad taste was one thing, but this went beyond it. (I mean not really, I was never going to cut them out. But it felt powerful to pretend I could). The more I thought about it, the less I was able to understand it. My friends were being just hatefully mean to me for no reason. They left their credit card to mitigate the shear meanness of it, but that wasn't really enough. Apparently Riley felt the same way. She picked up her menu.

"Yes, miss. We'd like a bottle of your most expensive red wine...and a bottle of your most expensive white wine. Uh...we'd like one of...let's say each of the appetizers. We'd also like two of your most expensive entrees and...let's say the catch of the day for us to share," she said, pointing to each item on the menu as the waitresses eyes got wider. Riley spoke pointedly, each word spilling out of her mouth like she was spitting out a razor blade. I liked the way she sounded, feeling my righteous indignation mirrored in her voice.

"Actually, we have a really nice white to pair with the fish..." The waitress attempted to say.

"Is it the most expensive white wine?"

"No but..."

"We want the expensive one. Our pallets are crazy sophisticated," she said and, despite my anger, I had to giggle, "Thanks." And then Riley handed the menus back to the waitress. The waitress looked a little bit dazed but nodded and walked away.

"Oh my god, you are so crazy!" I said once the waitress was gone. I was glad that this girl was on my side. I wanted to get even, but I wouldn't have even known where to start.

"I hope you don't mind me ordering for you, we are on a date after all," she said and I actually smiled.

"Not at all, as long as you promise to save room for dessert."

"Desserts," she said and we both laughed a little bit. We sat in silence for a few moments, just trying to come to terms with the new situation. Finally, I had an idea.

"Hey, do you just want to leave? I mean, they are going to charge them for the food anyway, let's just both go home," I suggested.

"Uh...No Ash. I appreciate the offer, but I am staying," she said, "First of all, I am nowhere near done here. Second, like I said, I cleared my schedule. I have nowhere else to be. Do you?"

"Well I could go back to the office I guess, but really no..." I replied, wondering what I could be doing more productive than this.

"Then fuck it," Riley responded, "Let's just take it easy and have the most expensive meal of our lives. You seem like good company, let's get back at them by enjoying our 'date.'" I tilted my head to the side and looked at Riley. What she said made sense. I nodded.

"Yeah, I guess so," I said, "You seem like more fun than paperwork"

"A ringing endorsement," she responded and I laughed. At that moment, the sommelier arrived with two bottles of wine. He seemed surprised that he was bringing two bottles for two people. But he popped the corks and we inspected them. He was about to pour the wine into the glasses.

"Woah there," Riley said, grabbing at the red wine bottle, "We can handle that part." She said. The sommelier looked at her like she was crazy.

"They usually do that kind of stuff for you."

"No, I usually do this stuff for me. He is going to fill it like a quarter of the way up so it can pretentiously 'breathe.' I want to get drunk on someone else's dime, I am filling my glass," she said, tilting the wine bottle up, "and yours to the top." And she poured out her wine until it was almost at the rim. The sommelier shook his head and walked away.

"I have work in the morning," I said, placing my hand over my glass. I really did.

"Don't make me drink alone Ash," she said, she started to pour the wine out of the bottle! It splashed against my hand and I quickly drew it back. Soon she was filling my glass just as she had hers. I wanted to be angry, but I just laughed at her boldness. She didn't try to convince me of anything, she just did what she wanted and expected me to get in line. I admired that.

"Well, you drive a hard bargain," I said, "But I guess I am in." Riley lifted her glass, very carefully, for a toast. I did the same.

"To...a dyke date I guess," Riley said and clinked her glass against mine. I laughed.

"To...that," I said. We brought our glasses up and both took deep drinks of the expensive (and tasty) wine. Riley didn't hold back, she downed her glass of wine, gulping it like water, and then set her glass back down.

Part 8

"Wow, I haven't pounded wine like that since college, and that was cheap stuff," Riley said when she finished, her eyes watering.

"That couldn't have been that long ago," I said, taking another big drink of my own wine. For some reason, I wanted to keep pace with her.

"I graduated...two years ago. But it feels longer," she said. The drink seemed to relax her some and she leaned back in the booth, "How about you?"

"How about me what?" I asked.

"How long ago did you graduate?" she asked, and then she smiled, "I guess that's my not-so-sneaky way of asking how old you are." I laughed.

"Oh wow, I am 34 so I guess I graduated about…11 years ago," I said, had it really been that long?

"Wow!" Riley said, "Wouldn't have guessed that."

"What do you mean?"

"Don't take this the wrong way, I am not saying you are childish or anything but…you don't look 34. I thought you were like 25 or 26 at the oldest."

"I can tell you are under 30, because no one over 30 ever takes being called 9 years younger than calendar age to be anything but a compliment," I said back. I felt a sort of warm glow that was a mixture of the expensive wine settling in my stomach and feeling flattered by the compliment. Maybe my "date" would give me a little ego boost, despite the obvious handicap.

Riley refilled her glass and then topped mine off with the remains of the bottle. I wondered how much money we'd just drunk in a couple of minutes. But I didn't care. I took another swig of the expensive wine and felt the effects already starting to occur.

"So where'd you go?" I asked.

"I'm right here," Riley said and then giggled a bit. She had really been attacking the wine and it sounded like it went right to her head. I laughed at her joke.

"No college, you said you haven't pounded wine since college, where was college? Party school? Hey no, judgment I went to state" I said. Riley actually laughed a little bit. She reached down her shirt between breasts and grabbed something. She pulled the chain of a necklace up over her hair and handed it across to me.

"Oh it was an absolute trip, but it wasn't a party," she said. I felt my brow furrow and I reached out and took the object that Riley offered. The chain was thin silver band, but the pendant was large. When I looked down I saw that it wasn't a pendant at all, but a ring. A class ring in fact, from Davis Bible College.

"Bible College?" I asked, raising my eyebrows. Riley laughed and nodded, taking the ring back from me.

"Yeah," she laughed, "I figured I stood out as a Davis alum from my modest dress, my humorless demeanor, and chaste behavior." She said and then to accentuate she took a big drink of wine. I laughed at her joke, but really couldn't ever see this punky looking girl at bible school.

"I can honestly say that was the last thing I expected. I would've been less surprised if you went to clown college," I responded. At around this moment, the waitress arrived with the first of our giant load of appetizers. We started eating immediately and the food was worth the price. Or at least the price to Kim and Eric.

"Well," Riley said as she finished off a shrimp, "My parents are both INSANELY conservatively Christian. It was choice between Bible College or no college." She explained.

"Not much of a choice," I said.

"Not for me, I needed out of that house. I didn't want to be married at 18 like half the girls at my church," she explained. I felt a sudden well of admiration for this girl. It must've been difficult to buck her tradition upbringing, even just a little bit, and go to school. That took courage. I looked up at Riley now, taking a sip of my wine, and considered her. She was young and a bit wild, but she was also funny, delightfully impulsive, and brave. Not to mention very pretty. I found that I liked her and wondered if Eric and Kim had not set us up as a joke, but maybe so that we could be friends. Of course, if that was the case, they could have just introduced us. Why all this play acting at romance? I didn't spend much time considering that possibility, the taste of wine on my tongue made me realize something.

"Where were you pounding wine at Bible College?" I suddenly asked. "I would figure it would be wall to wall true believers." Riley laughed and shrugged her shoulders.

"Yeah it pretty much was, except for my junior and senior years. When I was a junior another girl like me showed up as a freshman, Heather. We ditched the religious classes together and actually had fun. It was kind of like a a real college experience after that. And I was old enough to buy alcohol, so it was just a matter of finding a place to get drunk," she explained. I figured that that made some sense.

Part 9

[Listen to this song while reading]

"Judging by that wine glass and your professional demeanor, you weren't much of a partier in college," She said. I felt a little self-conscious and finished the last of my wine. I might not have had quite as much as Riley, but I was a lightweight. I wasn't feeling it too much yet, but I knew I would before long.

"I guess I wasn't," I said, "Every once in a while Kim would convince me to..."

"Kim as in Hot Kim? You've known her for like ten years?" she asked. It was still such a strange nickname, though I had to admit that Kim was a beautiful woman.

"Yeah, longer really," I said.

"Does this seem like...in character for her?' Riley said, switching back to our earlier guess as to our friends' motive. "Like I can't imagine Eric doing this, is Kim a schemer? I've only talked to her twice."

"No," I said, thinking about my friend, who was sweet and kind and sensitive, "No, not like her at all. She is a lovely person." I said, being more honest than maybe I should have.

"So weird," Riley said, placing some sort of fried puff ball into her mouth and chewing, "Oh God!" she said, spitting it back out into her napkin, "Not nearly as weird as that!" I laughed so loudly that people in other booths looked over and I quickly quieted, though I leaned in towards Riley and kept laughing.

"I think it was some sort of sea food," I said while laughing.

"I think it was locker room feet and burnt hair!" Riley said, causing me to laugh again, "god damn hipsters and their weird ass food." She finished ruefully.

"At least it's free," I said and Riley raised her glass. I found my glass of wine and the new bottle, and decided to join her.

I suppose it would be tedious to go over the conversation we held at dinner at length. Not to say that the conversation was tedious, far from it. Just, that the blow by blow is not necessarily essential to the story here. A few more appetizers came and eventually our gigantic meal arrived. There was far too much food to eat and soon we were both stuffed.

The whole while, we carried on a lively conversation. Mostly I spoke about work, because it was really the only thing that I had to talk about. I felt bad, like I was boring her and also driving home to myself that I had no real life. But Riley seemed genuinely interested both in my job and in me as a professional (as well as a person). She asked me for professional advice and I got the feeling that despite her slacker appearance, that she had large ambitions for herself. And the acuity of her questions indicated that she had the perceptiveness necessary to achieve those ambitions.

Regardless, I didn't need to worry too much if I was making boring conversation, as Riley spoke enough for two. I learned that Riley was one of six children, the youngest. I learned that she grew up in an outer suburb of the city and that her parents had nearly disowned her when they learned she took a job at a secular record label. She jokingly said that she couldn't tell if her father was angrier that she'd chosen to work in a "sinful" medium or that she had chosen a profession in a field ripe for extinction. Her mother, whom it was clear she hated, revered, and loved deeply all at the same time, had just feared for her soul. She explained that she convinced them that it would be both a chance to spread the word of God and also to learn transferrable business skills and they had relented. All of Riley's stories were uproariously funny, even the ones that should not have been. Despite the monopoly she placed on conversation (which grew more overwhelming she drank) I wished I could hear more about her. I found her absolutely fascinating and undeniably cool.

The whole while we were talking and eating we were also drinking. About an hour into our "date" we had ordered a third bottle of wine. This was a cheaper bottle (we decided to take it easy on Kim and Eric because we were having fun) but it was arguably stronger than the first two. By the time we both abandoned attempts to finish eating, we were both pretty well drunk. Riley suggested that, instead of buying a dessert, which we couldn't eat, that we head to the bar and "drink" our dessert. Normally, I would decline such an offer. I never much liked liquor. But I was already drunk and eager to extend my positive mood and Riley's attitude was absolutely contagious. So I agreed and we moved back. I can't remember if I had two or three shots of tequila before, I came to my fateful realization for the night, but I remember how it happened.

Riley and I were sitting on the far left side of the bar, we both had a shot of tequila in our hands, as I remember it, and I was laughing at something that she had said (though I can't recall exactly what it was, she made me laugh a lot that night). I was feeling more loose and uninhibited than I had in years. Maybe ever.

"Okay look," Riley said, "It is a simple sequence. First, the salt. Then the tequila. Then the lime. Last time you did it backwards, and you have to do it right."

"Will I not get drunker if I do it in the wrong order?" I asked playfully.

"No. And you'll prove once and for all that my dream of opening a drinking school is dead as I lack the capacity to teach drunks," she said and I smiled. She was standing up at the time, just barely resting her ass against the bar stool. She sort of towered over me as she instructed.

"Well I'd hate to do that!" I slurred, "Okay, tequila, lime, salt." I said. I can't remember if this was a joke or I really didn't remember.

"No! Salt, tequila, lime. Watch!" Riley said. She quickly licked salt off of her wrist, pounded a shot of tequila, and finished it off with squeeze of lime. Her face contorted in agony. Why do people do this? "See, easy."

"Right," I said, "Lime, Salt, and then Lime,"

"You didn't even remember tequila that time!" Riley laughed and then she pushed away from the bar, "Okay, do not drink that in the wrong order. Just wait for me. I am going to run to the little girl's room, I am going to come back and get another drink, and show you how this is done. Got it?"

"Got it. Get another drink, go to the bathroom, show me how it's done," I said, purposefully mixing the order this time (I promise). Riley laughed and slapped my arm playfully.

"You've got some weird ideas Ash. You figure out the bathroom on your own when the time comes," she said and then turned to walk towards the bathroom. As she walked away I found my eyes follow her. I noted the way her hair cascaded messily down her back, the feminine narrowness of her shoulders, the way her figure sloped down from her armpits to her thin waist, and then ballooned back out in an hourglass shape. The swell of her ass in her tight jeans and the way her legs looked long and delicate in the denim. In short, I was checking her out and found myself...liking what I saw.

Part 10

I guess I was drunk and normally I wouldn't have put much stock into those thoughts (I figured any woman could objectively respect the beauty of another woman's form, it didn't mean anything), but one idea in particular caused me to pause. As my eyes scanned over Riley's ass as it saw high and first in her pants, I had thought, "she's got an amazing butt, it looks like Kim's when she was in college."

At first, this idea barely registered. Just one thought amongst many. But then I began to think of how strange it was that I had decided to compare physical attributes of my new friend with that of my old friends. And as I thought about that, I realized that it hadn't been the only thing. I realized other thoughts I'd had during the course of the evening, "She has a lilting laugh, like Kim," and "She rubs her lower lip with the back of her thumb, like Kim," or perhaps most damning, "she has a dirty sense of humor, nothing like Kim." Even when Riley was nothing like Kim, I found myself making that the point of comparison. It was like I was using Kim as the measuring stick by which to gauge Riley. And as I thought of that, I realized it wasn't just Riley. I compared everyone to Kim. She was the universal constant.

I felt extremely strange coming to that realization and I placed my elbows on the bar, trying to figure out what it was, exactly, I was grasping at. Thinking about Kim made me remember why I was here, the "prank." But now drunk, and no longer horribly embarrassed, I no longer felt that this explanation for the situation made any sense. Strangely, the drinking had cleared my mind a bit, allowed me to look at the situation clearly. Kim wouldn't do something just to hurt me. She wouldn't have found it funny even if it happened by accident. Eric and Kim hadn't been pulling a prank. Hell, they left money on the table for us. So what were they doing?

Suddenly, my conversation with Kim earlier in the week, when she convinced me to go on this date, flooded back to me. And listening them in my memory, without denial and discomfort I had felt in the initial event, allowed me to hear things that I hadn't heard before.

Kim said: "I can't sit by while you choose to be miserable," and "I think that you always date...the wrong kind of people...and are miserable, that you think the absence of misery is happiness." She asked "Ash, how often do we see each other? How often do we talk?" Perhaps most importantly she'd said, "You are grasping for something here, with me, that my family and I just cannot provide for you...You need... you need more than I can give you as your best friend." And she summed it all up saying "I think you want something that you don't even know that you want and cannot understand."

I stood up quickly from the bar stool, almost losing my balance. The bartender looked over at me quizzically, perhaps wondering if I was alright. But the shot of adrenaline I felt now had done wonders to mitigate my drunkenness. I cannot completely or fully describe what I was feeling at that moment, the emotions were too chaotic. All I can say was that I felt an intense existential embarrassment that had attendant branches of fear, self-loathing, confusion, shame, and surprise.

I felt like some sort of feral animal, caught play-acting like a human being. I know that makes no sense, but that was the totality of my emotion. And, as an animal, I quickly slipped into fight or flight mode. And the only thing in the world that I wanted was to be away from this place. To go back to my home, close the door, and die. That is not youthful dramatics. At that moment, the weight of my life was unbearable and while I did not want my existence to cease, it felt like it would be easier if it did.

"I am on Kim and Eric's tab," I yelled, in a crackling voice, at the bartender. He turned to me, confused. He'd been speaking with someone else. I didn't care. I felt tears in my eyes, tears that I could not adequate explained, and I turned and ran towards the door. Still a little drunk, I bumped into chairs as I moved quickly. I reached the table where Riley and I had eaten, grabbed my purse, and then I quickly made my way for the door and out into the street.

It was cold outside and I could see my breath steaming out of my mouth as I stumbled out into the dark night air. It hadn't been that cold when I arrived, but early fall was turning to late fall without the sun, it grew cold. I didn't know what time it was, but I took a deep breath and steadied myself. Then I oriented myself towards my condo and started to walk.

I didn't get very far when I heard someone calling my name. For a split second, I know it is crazy, but I thought that it was Kim. But then I heard it again, "Hey Ash? Ash? Are you alright?" It said and now I recognized it as Riley's voice. I realized I'd just abandoned her in the bar. I turned quickly and she was standing about twenty yards behind me in the doorway to the restaurant.

"I..." I started but couldn't finish. I didn't even have any idea what I was going to stay. The urge to get away came over me again and I started to turn and walk away.

"Ash? What the Hell? Was it something I said? Hey hold on!" I heard Riley say. I just kept moving. I figured she'd go back inside and find someone else to talk to. I couldn't be company right now. Maybe she'd meet a man in there and at least it would be a happy story for her. Maybe this date would be a strange story she told her kids someday about how she met their father and I would be a little color thrown in.

"Ash stop, why are you running away? I wasn't trying to offend you, drink your fucking Tequila any way you want!" Riley said and now I heard her right behind me. Riley had run after me. I stopped walking, sighed, and dropped my head. I was going to have to actually tell her to go away. I turned toward Riley and she was standing about five feet behind me. The street was completely empty and it was now very dark. Riley was standing under a street light, leaning against the pole and it seemed like the rest of the world existed as an impenetrable blackness around the light. Riley had a concerned look on her face and had her arms crossed over her breasts in the cold.

"I'm...sorry," I said finally, I walked back towards Riley and stopped when I too was standing underneath the light, just next to her.

"You don't have to be sorry if you just tell me what I did?" Riley said, she sounded very concerned. I wonder if her sort of brash attitude, which I enjoyed, was off-putting to some people. Maybe she had a fear of driving people away and I was playing into that fear. I felt an intense guilt and shook my head.

"No, no you didn't do anything," I said, "It was me, it was all me." I didn't want to say any more than that. We stood in silence for a few minutes. I was shivering in the cold and I could see Riley shaking as well. Finally, she spoke.

"Hey I've gotten the old 'it's not you, it's me' thing at the end of a dozen dates," Riley joked, "but I usually get a little more explanation." I winced when she called it a date and her features softened. Riley looked at me deeply for several seconds, "What is it Ash? Come on, we've had fun tonight, we are kind of like friends already, let me know why you ran out of that place while we were laughing and having a good time. I can listen."

I considered for a moment just making something up, just some lie to cover over everything and get home. The desire to do this was so overwhelming that for a second I opened my mouth to explain that I was sick. But I looked into Riley's eyes. I could feel a sort of...I don't know, empathy or understanding pouring out of her. I could feel her sort of going out to me. And she was right we'd had fun that night, but more than that I'd felt some connection to her that I couldn't really understand. She deserved to know the truth, she was in the same boat as me. More importantly, I wanted to tell the truth. To get this realization out of my brain and out into the world.

"I..." I started and my voice sounded choked, but Riley nodded and looked at me inquisitively, "I realized tonight that I am...sexually attracted to my best friend Kim. I think I am infatuated with her," I finally managed to say. Riley jerked back like she'd been hit.

Part 11 (I Fell in Love with my Best Friend)

[Listen to this song while reading]

The effect on me was even greater. Ever since I'd had my sort of dawning of knowledge in the bar, I had avoided actually, explicitly thinking about what it was that I was thinking. I had sort of walled it up, one last ditch defense by my denial. But saying the words out loud made it undeniable. I desired my best friend, I wanted to love her and make love to her.

Thinking that caused a dozen scattered images to flitter through my brain, things that Kim had clearly noticed even when I did not. I remembered watching a movie with Kim in college and cuddling up extremely close to her, actually putting my head on her shoulder. I remembered going to the beach with her one year and conspicuously wiping sand off of her ass. I remembered driving to a concert with her once when Eric was sick and couldn't make it and actually saying that I wished it was always just the two of us. Perhaps most damning, I remembered her picking me up at the airport once after a long business trip, we'd hugged at I'd held her a little too long. I'd gone to kiss her on the cheek, but leaned too far and kissed the corner of my mouth. We laughed it off, but it hadn't totally been an accident.

Now, these were just a handful of moments across a relationship that spanned a decade and a half. Each event was a tiny little bit of my life that by itself was largely meaningless. I hadn't even realized that there was a pattern. But, now the first time thinking of these events cumulatively, I suddenly felt pathetic, transparent, and stupid. Obviously, Kim had seen these isolated events and discerned what I could not. She knew I loved her in a way that was far different from the way she loved me. And so she'd...tried to make me understand. Oddly, this made me both intensely ashamed but also made me love Kim even more. Not embarrassed or disgusted by me, she just tried to help me. That was the Kim I knew, not the prankster. But I was still pathetic.

Riley was still looking at me, her eyes wide and her mouth slightly ajar. She was still shivering, but her focus was entirely on me now. I realized I owed her a little bit more.

"I'm really sorry. I wasn't trying to leave you like that...I mean I was but it wasn't about you. I think that my friend realized that I had feelings for her and so she set me up on this date with you. I don't think it was a joke, I think she was trying to help me. But when I realized it, I just needed to leave. I didn't want to make you uncomfortable. I don't even know why they picked you, maybe they thought because you were young and sounded rebellious...I don't know. But I was just trying to leave before anything got awkward." I spilled it all out, trying to be truthful but to say as little about myself as possible. I noticed Riley's eyes drop and I figured that she understood. She was shaking her head. I felt dirty and ashamed. I hoped this meant I could now leave.

"It all makes sense," Riley whispered and a winced. Had she been able to tell I was attracted to women too? Was I the only one who didn't know? "The Christmas party," she said.

"What?" I asked. Riley looked up at me. I saw something familiar in her eyes, confusion or something different. She was taking deep breaths and gulping. What was going on?

"Last winter, at the office Christmas party," Riley said and then paused for a minute, not letting her eyes meet mine, "I got really drunk. I always get drunk in social situations. I always act the same, drunk or sober, but at least when I am drunk I don't feel embarrassed about it. Anyway, I got into a yelling match with some secretary from a different department and Eric had grabbed and pulled me into his office. Everyone got a laugh about it.

"Once we were back inside, Eric calmed me down, got me to realize that I was going to get myself fired. I was really pissed at him at first, but he was really sweet about everything. So I started talking to him about how I used to get in fights all the time when I was drinking in college and that got me reminiscing about college. You know how it is when you are drunk, and you just want to talk about stuff. And Eric was just fine to listen and everything. So I told him that when I was in school that Heather would keep me out of trouble, just like he was doing then.

"That got me talking about Heather, just general stuff, stories and everything. And I must've told him (I can't remember 100% if I told him, but I must've) about something that happened my senior year. Heather and I went out drinking and I got in a screaming match with some girl. As a result, we didn't get back to campus until late. Heather was only a sophomore so she still had a roommate. She didn't want to wake her roommate up, so I invited her stay in my room. Got back to the room and I passed out drunk on the bed.

Part 12

"So I woke up the next morning hung-over with Heather in my bed. But she wasn't just in my bed. When I woke up Heather was already awake. She was lying on my left side on her belly and her left arm was draped across me, she was actually holding my breast. And she was kissing my neck. So I sat up really quickly.

"'What are you doing?' I asked, or something like that. She looked kind of confused.

"'We got back last night and talked about fooling around. You said you wanted to. You brought it up. Then you passed out. I thought we could try it again today.'

"And I was shocked. I mean, I had no recollection of that at all. But I knew she was telling the truth. I knew that I had...feelings for

Heather. They were always just below the surface. We were so close." For a moment, Riley stopped talking and just looked down at the sidewalk below her feet. I heard a slight hitch in her voice. But she continued.

"And apparently I'd finally said something to act on it when I was drunk. And Heather hadn't just been into it then. She was still ready the next morning. I mean, it was the answer to my unasked for wish! I couldn't believe how lucky I was. How could Heather feel the same way?

"And she said…And I will never forget what she said, because she said, 'come on sunshine, I won't bite unless you ask.' She kind of laughed but I felt my blood run cold. My mother…She always called me 'sunshine.' It was an ironic nickname she gave me because I was such a blustery kid. And suddenly I wondered what my mother would think if she saw me like this. If I went any further. I could rebel against my parents by going to school or by dressing funny and swearing. Or even drinking. But lesbian sex… sexual purity was like THE primary belief of my parent's church. I had asked Heather to commit an abomination with me. And she would. And, I didn't think I believed in that. But my whole family believed it. And even though I pushed back against everything my parents stood for, my mother was still my model for womanhood. I still wanted...desperately wanted to be a woman like her. I knew that I wasn't, but I couldn't give up on the ideal of being like her. Even then I think I knew I couldn't be the woman my mother is, but I wasn't ready to accept it.

"So I told Heather that it was a joke or something. I said I didn't really want it. I tried to be gentle; I didn't mock her or anything. I just said it was a misunderstanding. She knew it was a lie. And worse, she'd exposed herself freely to me. She had the same upbringing that I did. And she had been willing to love me because I asked her to, and I couldn't follow through. She must've felt so...abandoned. We weren't ever really the same after that. I haven't talked to her since I graduated. I think she dropped out." There were tears rolling down Riley's cheeks as she recalled this memory. I felt for her, though I didn't have any experience to compare. I wanted to show her that I understood, I reached out and took her elbow. I cradled it gently and rubbed her arm with my thumb, trying to show her some affection.

"I must've said something to Eric and so when his wife said something about you...they just decided," Riley said. And the final piece of the puzzle now made sense.

"I am sorry if this hurts, I didn't want you to deal with any of this, I just want to leave, I am so sorry," I said. Riley sighed and shook her head.

"I live with this every day. Part of me always knew who I was. Maybe that was why I reacted so...I don't instantly to this date. Like why I jumped to being angry and defensive so fast. Fighting against who I am, you know?" I thought about Riley's words for a moment. I understood who she was and why she behaved the way she did. It made sense, even if it was terribly sad. But I felt less certain of myself. Where did my hang-up come from?

"I guess it was different for me," I said, "It wasn't just below the surface or anything. It was so deeply buried that I didn't even realize it myself. Kim almost came out and said it and I still didn't realize it. I just...I couldn't realize it." I was trying to explain to myself as much as to Riley

I couldn't claim to have any religious-tinged fear of same-sex attraction that stretched back to childhood. My family was not a church going group. I didn't have an overbearing, conservative mother who sought to keep a tight lid on sexual conformity. My mom was almost a hippie and while we rarely talked about sex, I knew she wouldn't have cared as long as I was happy. My father was not appreciably different. The only explanation I could find was that, from my earliest days, it had always been my outright goal in life to do everything to do everything the "right" way. And doing things the right way meant following the most conventional path to a happy and successful life. People were supposed to work hard in grade school, join clubs and sports, apply to impressive colleges, go to a very impressive university, get an impressive job, and then work like crazy. I did all those things.

And one thing that women were supposed to do was find a man they loved and marry him. And so I never questioned that that was what I was supposed to do. And when it didn't work out, I considered it a failing on my part. I was doing something wrong. It just...it never occurred to me that I had set one goal that was unachievable. I couldn't fall in love with a man and marry him, but because my heart (and my body) didn't want that. I needed something different. I hoped that Riley could understand.

"It was something that just wasn't one of the things that was supposed to be 'Me' so I didn't think about it. Like I actually repressed it. It wasn't just waiting for a chance to get out. It was like it didn't exist. Like I didn't really have sexuality. I didn't even have the first inkling of awareness of it until tonight."

"What made you realized it tonight," Riley asked, her brows furrowed. I looked at her, this woman I had spent the evening with. She was funny, quick, outrageous, and brave (though maybe not as brave as I'd first believed, she was vulnerable too, which was alluring). And I was learning that she was sweet, insightful, and caring. I looked at the gentle curve of her cheek, the brightness of her blue eyes, the long, delicate lashes above them. I saw the thick, full pinkness of her lips (quivering a bit in the cold). I found that my body felt like it was vibrating, my limbs felt weak, and my heart was simultaneously in my throat and at the bottom of my stomach, pounding. I felt an electrical feeling all over, something I'd never felt before. An anticipation for something, anything. My inner thoughts were a half-formed riotous requiem for a barrier that was about to break.

"It..."I started to explain, but found that my words failed me. The final dam had been broken. I had torn away all the defenses of a lifetime and suddenly I didn't have anything to hold me back. 34 years of longing was too much to hold back. And now there was this person in front of me, finally, reminding me of where that desire came from and where it was directed. I closed my eyes, turned my neck slightly to the side, and leaned forward. My body now did the work that my brain could not comprehend, urging my being forward towards oblivion or a new me. And both.

I felt my lips press softly against Riley's. Her lips were slightly cool and were pillowy soft. They were just slightly damp and thick and my two lips bracketed her lower lip carefully in an easy lock. The external sensation of my lips pressed against hers was absolutely lovely. But it was not entirely alien. It was a sweet, almost chaste kiss. But internally, the physical power of the kiss was overwhelming, beyond even the intense emotional effects.

Part 13

I had heard people talk about the way a kiss, especially a first kiss felt. I had felt "nice" kisses but I always thought that further descriptions were just wishful, romantic nonsense. If anything, I had underestimated the power. Inside my chest, my heart fluttered lightly, course blood quickly through my body. Along my arteries and all my nerves, electrical impulses seemed to shoot. Every spot on my body felt like it was pulsing with raw energy and the overall whole felt like something more. Despite this charge, my body felt loose, relaxed like I'd never felt before. In fact, I felt like my body had melted into Riley's kiss. I lacked any form except for the way my lips conformed to hers.

When her lips responded to my kiss, matching my lock, I felt my knees grow weak and my head grew foggy. The rest of the world sort of faded away. Everything that was not contained within the skirt-shaped light above our heads was an abstraction, an idea. The only thing in the entire world was us, shivering slightly in the cold. Our lips were pressed together and I could smell wine mixed with perfume. My hand still rested gently on Riley's elbow and we leaned towards one another but our bodies didn't touch. It was...perfect and we stayed that way for a long while.

Finally, our kiss broke and I opened my eyes as I pulled away slightly. Riley's eyes were still closed and she looked angelic, innocent. Eventually her large blue eyes fluttered open, but her body stayed relatively limp and relaxed.

"I've never had a kiss like that," I said.

"Me neither," Riley responded, if felt strange to talk. Like we'd become something different than we'd been just moments before. But what did we do now? I knew what my body wanted. But what did Riley want? I decided to be forthright.

"Do you want to...come back to my place?" I asked nervously. Part of me knew she would say yes, but I was still not comfortable in all of this. Beyond the fact that none of it felt real. Riley cooed slightly rested her head on my shoulder.

"I only ever had this kind of opportunity once before and I blew it," she said, "I don't want to blow it again. My apartment is only two blocks away." She lifted her head again and looked at me. She had this playful smirk on her face and I must've returned it. In an instant, Riley's hands slipped down off of my body. She quickly grabbed my hand and started to run. I didn't even think, I just followed after her.

We ran pell mell down the street, heedless of everything else in the universe. I could hear Riley laughing as she ran and watched the exquisite form of her body as she moved. I laughed along with her and enjoying the ride. We sprinted back past the restaurant where we'd met. And then across a side street. Riley picked up speed now, running faster and my 9-year-older workaholic legs struggled to keep up. We ran through another intersection and I heard a car horn blare at us but didn't see it.

In few moments we ran up to tan brick building. Riley threw the door open and we ran inside. There was a somewhat large lobby with four elevators, two on either side. Riley ran to the middle of the room and pushed the button, jerking me across the floor panting and giggling and I flopped around wildly. The elevator did not instantly arrive and so she pulled me gasping, farther into the room. She opened up a set of doors.

"Just the second floor," she said and started to drag me up the stairs. The fact that we were so close gave me a second wind and I pounded up the winding staircase. A few seconds later we spilled out onto the second floor of the apartment building. Riley moved quickly to a door, presumably hers, and stopped.

"Shit," she said.

"What?"

"Let my purse and keys at the restaurant," she explained. I felt a draining feeling. This was going to fall apart. What was I doing? "Fuck it," she said and dropped to her knees. I wondered if she expected me to make love to her right there (and I was tempted). But she lifted up her welcome mat and retrieved a key. She quickly got up, slammed it into her lock and opened the door.

Part 14 (Way too much sex)

She turned the lights on as I stumbled into the room. It was a small studio apartment with cheap furniture but a big window opening up on the street just fifteen feet below. Riley had a large sofa that sat along the wall a few feet from the front door. It was a converter bed and was clearly the place where she slept. It was open and the sheets were a bit disheveled. She hadn't planned to bring her male date home it seemed. I didn't care if it was messy. I wanted on that bed.

Before I could do anything, Riley took my arm and swung me around. She wrapped her arms around my waist and pulled me into her body. Once again I felt our hips and our breasts press together.

I closed my eyes and felt Riley's tongue play across my lips. The excitement was building now. We were both hurtling toward something and that realization made us want it faster, now! Our kiss was wilder this time, our mouths moving chaotically. Without realizing I was acting, I felt my arms move around Riley's body and my fingers felt her lower back, her shoulders, her neck was we passionately embraced. We were both completely wild with lust now, our novice uncertainty couldn't hold us back. Our bodies had taken over and we were going to keep acting until we achieved something that would give us peace.

Out of the cold and into Riley's cramped, overheated apartment, I instantly felt hot. Of course, my contact with Riley might've had something to do with that as well. I pushed back slightly from Riley and quickly slipped one arm out of my coat. I then sort of flung the whole thing off quickly and turned back to continue kissing Riley. But she'd acted quickly. While my arms were outstretched her hand had flown to my body. Her fingers found my buttons and was rapidly opening my shirt. I moaned slightly and let her continue. She untucked my shirt from my pants and then flung it off over my shoulders. I let my blouse slide off my arms. Now I was exposed save for my black demi-bra.

Riley looked at my body, the flare of my hips, the swell of my breasts, my dimple of a bellybutton, now all fully exposed. I could see the desire in her eyes and I felt so sexy in that moment, something I never recalled feeling before. But Riley had a need to see more. She reached forward and slipped her fingers into the top of my left bra cup. I gasped as I felt her warm fingers and cool nails press into my skin. Then Riley quickly pulled down, popping my breast out of the cup and into the exposed air of her home.

I gasped at the feeling, less from the physical sensation than from the emotional impact of exposure. A part of my body that I rarely exposed was free. For the first time in my life, my breast was not dutifully exposed while having obligatory sex with a man I did not care for. I was desperate for Riley to see all of my body. It felt...good.

I didn't have long to gaze. In a second, Riley bent over at her waist, her mouth open. In a split second, my nipple was no longer exposed, it was engulfed her mouth. I grunted (I admit it) and my legs shook a little. I couldn't keep my balance and I felt back against the front door. Riley didn't seem to notice. I heard a soft moan emanate from her throat as she continued to kiss my nipple. Her hot, wet tongue moved thickly across the taut skin of my nipple, flicking it and playing with it gently.

"Oh Jesus!" I moaned and closed my eyes. The sensation was just too intense to bear. Riley's face sank into the soft flesh of my breast and her attentions on my nipple were intensely passionate. It seemed like all of the nerves in my body were routed through that nipple and each tiny movement of her tongue pulled strings in my knees and shoulders, causing me to slump.

Riley began to suck gently on my nipple and I opened my eyes. I looked down across my chest. I could see Riley's big, beautiful eyes looking up at me from there. Her irises, generally very bright, shone with a kind of brilliance I didn't think was possible. Seeing those big blue lights shining up at me increased the ardor of the moment. I needed something more.

It was at this moment I realized that, in a few seconds, I was going to be completely naked and Riley would still be fully clothed. I desperately wanted to see her body. Even the thought of doing so made my stomach flip. I looked at Riley, whose eyes were now closed, concentrating on all of her tasks (and still doing an amazing job).

I noticed that her feet were sort of far forward, her butt sticking backwards. She was a bit off balanced. I had a fun little idea.

In one quick motion, I moved my hands up towards Riley's neck, grabbed her collar and pulled it wide over on her t-shirt, and gave her a gentle shove with my wrists. Riley tottered and then started to fall backwards. My nipple popped out of her mouth, "Woah!" she said as she completely lost balance. As she fell, I held on tight to her shirt. It popped up over her head and a moment later, Riley fell onto her back on the pull-out sofa, giggling, and wearing only a pink bra above her waist.

"You think you are pretty clever," she said laughing and I smiled back at her. I tossed her t-shirt at her and she caught it and threw it on the floor. "Come here," she said, hooking her index finger at me. I wanted to go after her right then. She looked so amazing. Her body, what I could see of it, was just as lovely as I'd imagined. She was soft and delicate, with exquisite curves. Her small breasts sat up high on her chest as she sat on the bed.

"I showed you mine, show me yours," I demanded, pointing to my breasts. Her eyes followed my finger and I saw her sort of get a dreamy smile when she looked at me.

"I don't think my breasts compare to yours, even if I take the bra off," she said and licked her lip.

"I will judge that," I responded. Riley seemed to want to do it and, without further comment, she reached behind her back and unhooked her bra. In a moment, she slid it off of her small body and threw it on the floor.

"So pretty," I said without thinking the instant she removed it. Her small breasts still sat high on her chest, as though she hadn't removed her bra (ah youth!) and had the perfect, tear drop shape that everyone wants. Her nipples were small, and extremely pink, standing out beautiful on her creamy white skin. They looked like they would taste lovely, popped into my mouth.

"You think so?" Riley asked, actually sounding a bit reticent.

"You are the most beautiful woman I have ever seen," I said and in that moment, I absolutely meant it. I'd never felt desire to possess anything as much as I wanted Riley's body. Riley smiled broadly.

Now Riley was lying on her back on her bed, wearing nothing but a pair of pink boy-short panties. Her legs were still spread and I could see a small patch of dark pink in the center of her panties. Riley was extremely wet. In fact, I could already smell her scent on the air. It was surprising both how potent her pheromones seemed to be and also how much I enjoyed it. I'd never liked the smells of sex (or sounds, or tastes...etc.) before. But Riley's sharp, but delectable aroma filled my nostrils and made my mouth water.

Beyond that, now that she was almost naked, I could see her whole body in its natural state. She was thin, she had long, somewhat bony arms and a surprisingly round ass, and her breasts were perfectly proportional. Somehow, she was more than the sum of her parts. She looked so innocent and sexy at the same time. I couldn't believe how badly I wanted her.

I was near her feet now, and I decided that I desperately needed to kiss her again.

As I scooted forward, I was surprised to find my pants slipping off my hips. In fact, Riley's toes had gotten so close to my skin that they were pulling my panties down as well! By the time my face was hovering a few inches above Riley's my pants and underwear were down around my knees! I was essentially naked.

"Cute trick, Monkey Toes," I said and Riley giggled.

"Oh god, please don't call me that while we're..." she said and then I laughed too. I figured it was too late now to be modest. I shift my weight from one knee and then the other, and quickly took my pants off and threw them on the floor. I was completely naked now. I could see Riley trying to look around me and realized that she wanted to see what I looked like entirely naked. I felt flattered and decided to oblige. I leaned forward and gave her a quick kiss on the cheek and then got up on my knees between her legs again.

Part 15

My eye lids split open the next morning as sunlight streamed through a window. The light was so bright that I couldn't see anything. For a moment, I had absolutely no idea where I was or what I was doing. I had a slight headache and a somewhat strange taste in my mouth. I remembered that I had been drinking the previous night. I then had three realizations in a row. First, I remembered who I had been with the night before. Second, my eyes cleared and I could see Riley asleep, facing me just a few inches away. Third, I could feel her body against mine. We were intertwined as we had been the whole night.

What had we done! For a moment I felt a cold panic. I hadn't really realized the previous night that I'd been drunk. But now, in the light of day with the headache and the girl I barely knew to prove it, I realized that I'd been making some rather unexpected decisions. Before I could fully process what I was thinking, my first instinct was to just get away. Something strange had happened and I wanted to be alone, in my condo, to think about it. Figure out what it meant. But, before I had the chance to attempt an escape, I realized that Riley was essentially on top of me. It would be impossible to leave without waking her. I settled back into the bed, my heart and brain pounding the same rhythm.

I found myself staring at Riley's sleeping face, trying to make sense of it. I now remembered the way she'd looked the night before, her features flush with sexual desire. I saw her innocent, sleeping face now. No matter what, I'd crossed some sort of barrier the previous night. It was no longer possible for me to pretend that I was not attracted to Riley. Or to women in general. I could not deny I was lesbian. She looked so beautiful, her body felt so...right against mine. That I knew it was the truth. Now, sober, that realization seemed even stranger than it had the night before.

I still hadn't figured out anything beyond that fact when I saw Riley's eyes start to flutter open. I held my breath, trying not to wake her. For some reason, I was nervous about it. I don't know what I expected.

Maybe she would be angry or ashamed. She'd pushed away her friend from college after a night of drinking got out of hand. Maybe I was in for a rejection as well. My efforts were in vain, after a few moments, Riley's beautiful blue eyes were looking right at me. She seemed confused for a moment, and then smiled sheepishly.

"Uh...Good morning," she said and then laughed nervously.

"Morning," I replied. Her eyes moved away from mine, unable to meet my gaze. I was glad, I felt so awkward. But neither of us dared moved, our naked bodies remained tangled together and I could feel her muscles move slightly against mine. After several agonizing minutes, Riley's gaze returned to me.

"Sorry, just not used to this," she apologized. I shrugged a little.

"Waking up with a girl?" I asked.

"Well yeah, obviously that. But I mean, waking up after a drunken hookup and having the person still in my bed," she explained, "It is a little weird." I remembered my attempt to bolt.

"Well I guess that shows how men are different from women, it would have being so disrespectful for me to just abandon you," I said, trying to lend a knowing air to my voice. Riley seemed to pick up on it.

"Couldn't get out from under me eh?" she asked.

"Not for lack of trying," I said and now she laughed, this time without anxiousness. I loved the way she sounded, that musical, feminine quality of her laugh and I joined her. Riley rested her head on the pillow next to me, looking at me with some concentration.

"So what happened?" she asked after a long pause. It seemed like a simple question, but wasn't. I gave the simple answer.

"We had sex," I said. Riley made a raspberry noise with her tongue.

"Well yeah," she said, "But I mean...What happened? One second we were drinking and being friends, the next we were baring our sexual dirty laundry, and then all of the sudden we were back here having sex. Like incredible sex." I blushed at her description, but it was accurate. The best sex I'd ever had. And very sudden.

"I don't know," I responded honestly, but the more I thought of it, my mind now sober, the more it made sense. Well, some kind of sense. So I decided to share it with her, "I think our friends realized that we wanted something that we'd hidden from ourselves. And last night, in an unguarded moment, we'd both been exposed at the same time. We both, at least for the night, accepted what we wanted and were surprised to find someone else who wanted the same thing. And we grabbed onto one another both because we knew what the other was feeling and because we knew that if we stopped then, if we backed down, we would just hide from ourselves again. We both knew without thinking or saying anything that...if we stopped then we might bury ourselves forever." It was the only explanation I had, and it felt so right in my mind.

"Thank you," Riley said after a long moment. I shook my head slightly.

"Why?" I asked. I hadn't done anything that I could think of that deserved thanks.

"I think you are right about last night. And I don't think I could've done that without you. And I don't just mean the obvious, like that I couldn't have had sex without another person. I mean, I don't think I could've gone through with doing anything with anyone, except for you. Someone who was feeling and thinking the same things."

"Well then thank you," I responded, "Because I feel the same way." I leaned forward now and kissed Riley gently on the lips. It felt like the only thing to do. Our eyes closed, it felt much like our first kiss the previous night. Chaste but somehow sexual, gentle but powerful. I felt my body begin to react and I could feel Riley respond as well. Slowly, our kiss broke. We looked at each other again for several minutes, just smiling like two kids in love for the first time.

"What does this mean? Like for me...or for...us?" Riley asked after a long while. I'd been thinking about the same thing but lacked the courage to ask. I let out a sigh.

The Final Chapter

"I don't know. I know, for me, this means I can no longer delude myself. I know that I am a lesbian woman and I know, from last night, that it is right for me. Nothing ever felt as right as last night," I said, Riley blushed and nodded, "But I learned last night that I have some complicated feelings for my best friend that I've never really come to terms with. I know that those feelings can't go anywhere, Kim is not a lesbian. But I have to sort of get a handle on those feelings now that I recognize them. I don't know what that means for us..." It was difficult to say. I wanted to just tell Riley I loved her and to have my story end with a happily ever after, but life is not that easy. Even after a single night I had real affection for Riley, I shared a bond with her that even Kim and I did not have. But that didn't mean that I knew anything more than that. Hell, I really did barely know this girl who was 9 years my junior.

"I still can't imagine what my mother would say, if she knew," Riley said after a long pause. I realized that her life was no simpler than mine. I rubbed my hand, gently across Riley's arm and gave her some support, "I know I am not going to Hell for last night. I know that because I know that there is no such place as a lake of fire and if there was, I wouldn't go there for doing something natural. But it is hard to just turn that off. I mean I believed it for so long." Riley sort of stared past me as she spoke. I knew she was trying to say the same thing I was. I decided to just come out and say it.

"It is too early to know," I said, "My life changed completely in the last 12 hours. All sense of predictability is gone." Riley's eyes focused and she smiled again.

"So what do we do? I mean I always just did whatever I was told to do. How do I live if I am not living my mother's life?" She asked. I wondered the same thing. What was my life if it wasn't the mystical vision of normality that I'd created for myself so long ago? Strangely, that thought was comforting. I felt a freedom from constraint that I couldn't describe. My life, just like Riley's mother's life, was irrevocably broken. Whatever we made now would be whatever it was.

"Well," I said smiling, "Maybe we just live today like we did last night. Let's not make any plans or bind ourselves to anything we can't bear. Let's just do today what feels right for today and assume that it will lead to something right tomorrow." It was the only possible decision and Riley nodded back, her face looking without worry.

"What feel right at this minute?" she said, and as she spoke, she moved her right leg slightly. I felt the smooth, hot skin of her thigh rub across my pussy and I gasped slightly. My body tingled. I moaned slightly and looked at Riley. She looked so beautiful and I remembered the way she made me feel the night before. I realized that she was the only person in the world, at that moment, who knew who I really was. I spoke without thought.

"I don't want to say something that goes beyond this moment. I am not trying to plan out a future I can't possibly yet imagine. But I need to tell you that now, at this moment, I love you. And no matter what the future brings, if this is our last moment together, I will love you forever in this moment. What feels right, at this moment, is to show you how much I love you." I leaned forward now, closed my eyes and pressed my lips to Riley's cheek. My lips melted into her soft skin and I heard her gasp slightly. Her breath was in my ear and I knew that her mouth was right against my cheek.

"I love you too," she whispered, and then turned her face toward mine. I turned to meet her. In a moment, our eyes closed and our mouths met. Opposed to the exhilarating novelty of our first kiss or the quenchless passion of our later embraces the night before, this kiss had something else. A genuine tenderness. I felt Riley's lips on my mouth and the slightest hint of her tongue and felt a comfort from her. I wrapped my arms around her, pulling her tighter into me. Our breasts, still unclad from the previous night, pushed together and I felt the sticky warmth of her body.

For several minutes we just lay there, naked in one another's arms, our mouths pressed together. Occasionally, I would open my mouth and her tongue would find mine. But even this was gentle, sweet more than ardent. I thought of how different it felt to kiss Riley while I was sober, to have complete control over myself. But even with that control, to know that this was what I wanted. In some ways, it was better than the previous night.

I felt my body start to respond to our embrace and to our kisses. Just because we were calmer did not mean that to kiss Riley was any less arousing. In fact, our loving embrace felt even more exciting. I felt my pussy start to grow wet from the excitement. Perhaps more importantly, I could feel Riley's pussy dripping onto my thigh. She was aroused as well. And it created some sort of virtuous cycle. My arousal turned her on, just like her arousal turned me on. My excitement drove her excitement higher and vice versa.

And then we had sex again.

Riley collapsed on top of me as our orgasms faded. We were both breathing heavily and we lay together. She buried her face in my breasts and I wrapped my arms around her. For a long while we just laid that way, together and satisfied. The afterglow of our orgasm felt more intimate that it had the previous night, perhaps because we'd shared them. I played gently with her hair for a while and felt no overwhelming need to talk to think as I had before. Everything made sense and I felt so content. I could tell by the way that Riley felt against me that she was feeling the same thing. After half an hour, I almost fell back asleep. But then Riley spoke.

"Well, I have to get up and eat," Riley said comfortably. It didn't seem like we needed anymore explanations, we felt at peace, "come on I will make you breakfast." I kissed her one more time as she rolled off of me. She got up and walked across the room and I enjoyed the sight of her naked body walking away from me, the toned features of her butt and the gentle curves of her body. I reached over to grab my phone as I sat up. I hadn't called into work, and I wondered if I was in trouble. I would tell them I was sick.

All I had was a single text. From Kim. I opened it quickly and read it, "Oh my God!" I said, "You have to hear this!" Riley was almost to the kitchen area of her apartment, but she turned back and looked at me.

"What?" she asked.

"Kim wrote, 'I checked my account balance this morning. Your dinner cost Eric and I $421.74. You better still be on that date!'" I looked up from my phone at Riley. Her eyes got wide and then we both started to laugh. How much did each bottle of wine cost? Eventually our laughter died and Riley shook her head.

"I never expected that!" Riley said and I thought of her devil-may-care attitude and how it had drawn me to her. Of course she hadn't expect it, that was what made her Riley, "We will have to pay them back." She finished, showing there was no malice in her carelessness. I smiled at her and felt my affection growing.

"I don't think we ever can," I said and I got up from the bed to eat breakfast with my blind date. We'd solve all our problems later.

Is this a new beginning? I feel like I can get used to morning like this!

I think I have fallen in love on my first blind date.

The End.

www.ingramcontent.com/pod-product-compliance
Lightning Source LLC
Chambersburg PA
CBHW072215070526
44585CB00015B/1350